# CLASSICS

## *Illustrated* ®

## William Shakespeare
# HAMLET

essay by
Debra Doyle, Ph.D.

**STUDY GUIDE**

Hamlet

art by Alex Blum
adaptation by Sam Willinsky

Classics Illustrated: Hamlet © Twin Circle Publishing Co.,
a division of Frawley Enterprises; licensed to First Classics, Inc.
All new material and compilation © 1997 by Acclaim Books, Inc.

Dale-Chall R.L.: 8.5

ISBN 1-57840-006-6

Acclaim Books, New York, NY
Printed in the United States

**STUDY GUIDE**

# HAMLET

**H**AMLET WAS CALLED HOME TO DENMARK FROM GERMANY BY THE SUDDEN DEATH OF HIS FATHER, THE KING. ON HIS RETURN TO THE ROYAL CASTLE AT ELSINORE, HAMLET WAS SHOCKED TO FIND THAT HIS MOTHER HAD WAITED ONLY A FEW WEEKS AFTER HER HUSBAND'S DEATH BEFORE MARRYING AGAIN...THIS TIME TO CLAUDIUS, THE LATE KING'S BROTHER. BY THIS MARRIAGE, CLAUDIUS WAS ABLE TO SEIZE THE THRONE WHICH RIGHTFULLY BELONGED TO HAMLET. HAMLET WAS DEEPLY GRIEVED BY HIS FATHER'S DEATH AND EQUALLY BITTER OVER HIS MOTHER'S HASTY REMARRIAGE.

**NOW, ON WITH THE PLAY.**

ILLUSTRATED BY
ALEX A. BLUM

INSIDE THE ROYAL CASTLE, HAMLET SITS ALONE, GIVING VOICE TO HIS GRIEF AND BITTERNESS...

O, THAT THIS TOO TOO SOLID FLESH WOULD MELT, THAW AND RESOLVE ITSELF INTO A DEW; OR THAT THE EVERLASTING HAD NOT FIX'D HIS CANON 'GAINST SELF-SLAUGHTER! O GOD! O GOD! HOW WEARY, STALE, FLAT, AND UNPROFITABLE SEEM TO ME ALL THE USES OF THIS WORLD! FIE ON IT! AH FIE! 'TIS AN UNWEEDED GARDEN, THAT GROWS TO SEED; THINGS RANK AND GROSS IN NATURE POSSESS IT MERELY. THAT IT SHOULD COME TO THIS! BUT NOT TWO MONTHS DEAD! NAY, NOT SO MUCH, NOT TWO; SO EXCELLENT A KING; THAT WAS, TO THIS, HYPERION TO A SATYR; SO LOVING TO MY MOTHER, THAT HE MIGHT NOT BETEEM THE WINDS OF HEAVEN VISIT HER FACE TOO ROUGHLY, HEAVEN AND EARTH! MUST I REMEMBER? WHY, SHE WOULD HANG ON HIM, AS IF INCREASE OF APPETITE HAD GROWN BY WHAT IT FED ON; AND YET, WITHIN A MONTH-LET ME NOT THINK ON 'T. FRAILTY, THY NAME IS WOMAN! A LITTLE MONTH, OR ERE THOSE SHOES WERE OLD WITH WHICH SHE FOLLOWED MY POOR FATHER'S BODY, LIKE NIOBE, ALL TEARS, 'WHY, SHE, EVEN SHE, 'O GOD! A BEAST THAT WANTS DISCOURSE OF REASON WOULD HAVE MOURN'D LONGER, 'MARRIED WITH MY UNCLE, MY FATHER'S BROTHER, BUT NO MORE LIKE MY FATHER THAN I TO HERCULES; WITH A MONTH, 'ERE YET THE SALT OF MOST UNRIGHTEOUS TEARS HAD LEFT THE FLUSHING IN HER GALLED EYES, SHE MARRIED. IT IS NOT, NOR IT CANNOT COME TO GOOD: BUT BREAK, MY HEART, FOR I MUST HOLD MY TONGUE!

A MOMENT LATER, HORATIO, MARCELLUS, AND BERNARDO ENTER AND TELL HAMLET ALL THAT HAD HAPPENED THE NIGHT BEFORE...

I WILL WATCH TONIGHT; PERCHANCE 'T WILL WALK AGAIN.

MY FATHER'S SPIRIT IN ARMS. ALL IS NOT WELL; I DOUBT SOME FOUL PLAY; WOULD THE NIGHT WERE COME. TILL THEN SIT STILL, MY SOUL; FOUL DEEDS WILL RISE THOUGH ALL THE EARTH OVERWHELM THEM TO MEN'S EYES.

MEANWHILE, LAERTES, SON OF THE KING'S CHIEF ADVISOR, POLONIUS, READIES HIMSELF TO TRAVEL TO FRANCE. BEFORE GOING, HE WARNS HIS SISTER, OPHELIA, NOT TO RETURN HAMLET'S LOVE FOR HER. POLONIUS ENTERS AND CAUTIONS HIS SON AS TO HIS BEHAVIOR WHILE IN FRANCE...

GIVE YOUR THOUGHTS NO TONGUE, NOR ANY UNPROPORTION'D THOUGHT HIS ACT; ...THIS ABOVE ALL: TO THINE OWN SELF BE TRUE, AND IT MUST FOLLOW, AS THE NIGHT THE DAY, THOU CANST NOT BE FALSE TO ANY MAN. FAREWELL; MY BLESSING SEASON THIS IN THEE.

AFTER LAERTES LEAVES, POLONIUS ALSO WARNS OPHELIA AGAINST RETURNING HAMLET'S LOVE...

DO NOT BELIEVE HIS VOWS; I WOULD NOT, IN PLAIN TERMS, FROM THIS TIME FORTH HAVE YOU GIVE TALK WITH THE LORD HAMLET.

THE FOLLOWING DAY, POLONIUS SETS THE STAGE FOR HIS SCHEME. HAMLET, COMPLETELY UNAWARE OF THE PEOPLE ABOUT HIM, ENTERS. HE IS IN DEEP THOUGHT AND IS CONTEMPLATING SUICIDE...

TO BE, OR NOT TO BE: THAT IS THE QUESTION: WHETHER 'TIS NOBLER IN THE MIND TO SUFFER THE SLINGS AND ARROWS OF OUTRAGEOUS FORTUNE, OR TO TAKE ARMS AGAINST A SEA OF TROUBLES, AND BY OPPOSING END THEM. TO DIE, TO SLEEP--NO MORE; AND BY A SLEEP TO SAY WE END THE HEART ACHE AND THE THOUSAND NATURAL SHOCKS THAT FLESH IS HEIR TO; 'TIS A CONSUMMATION DEVOUTLY TO BE WISH'D; TO DIE; TO SLEEP; TO SLEEP, PERCHANCE TO DREAM; AYE, THERE'S THE RUB; FOR IN THAT SLEEP OF DEATH WHAT DREAMS MAY COME, WHEN WE HAVE SHUFFLED OFF THIS MORTAL COIL, MUST GIVE US PAUSE; THERE'S THE RESPECT THAT MAKES CALAMITY OF SO LONG LIFE: FOR WHO WOULD BEAR THE WHIPS AND SCORNS OF TIME, TH' OPPRESSOR'S WRONG, THE PROUD MAN'S CONTUMELY, THE PANGS OF DISPRIZ'D LOVE, THE LAW'S DELAY, THE INSOLENCE OF OFFICE, AND THE SPURNS THAT PATIENT MERIT OF TH' UNWORTHY TAKES, WHEN HE HIMSELF MIGHT HIS QUIETUS MAKE WITH A BARE BODKIN? WHO WOULD FARDELS BEAR, TO GRUNT AND SWEAT UNDER A WEARY LIFE, BUT THAT THE DREAD OF SOMETHING AFTER DEATH, THE UNDISCOVER'D COUNTRY FROM WHOSE BOURN NO TRAVELLER RETURNS, PUZZLES THE WILL AND MAKES US RATHER BEAR THOSE ILLS WE HAVE THAN TO FLY TO OTHERS THAT WE KNOW NOT OF? THUS CONSCIENCE DOES MAKE COWARDS OF US ALL; AND THUS THE NATIVE HUE OF RESOLUTION IS SICKLIED O'ER WITH THE PALE CAST OF THOUGHT, AND ENTERPRISES OF GREAT PITCH AND MOMENT WITH THIS REGARD THEIR CURRENTS TURN AWRY, AND LOSE THE NAME OF ACTION.--SOFT YOU NOW, THE FAIR OPHELIA!--NYMPH, IN THY ORISONS BE ALL MY SINS REMEMBER'D.

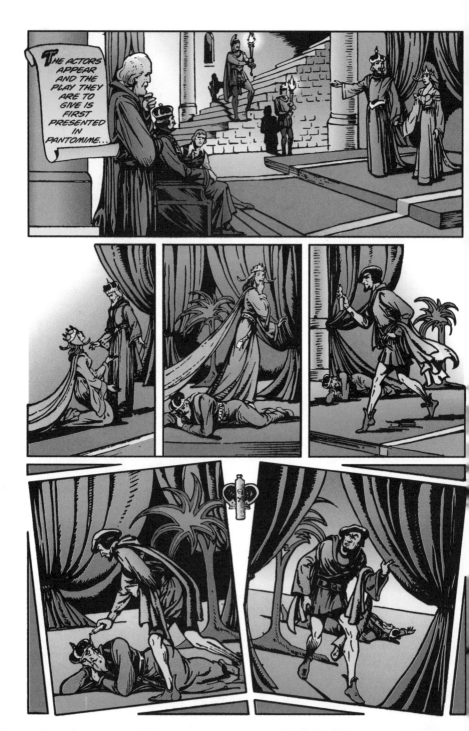

THE ACTORS APPEAR AND THE PLAY THEY ARE TO GIVE IS FIRST PRESENTED IN PANTOMIME...

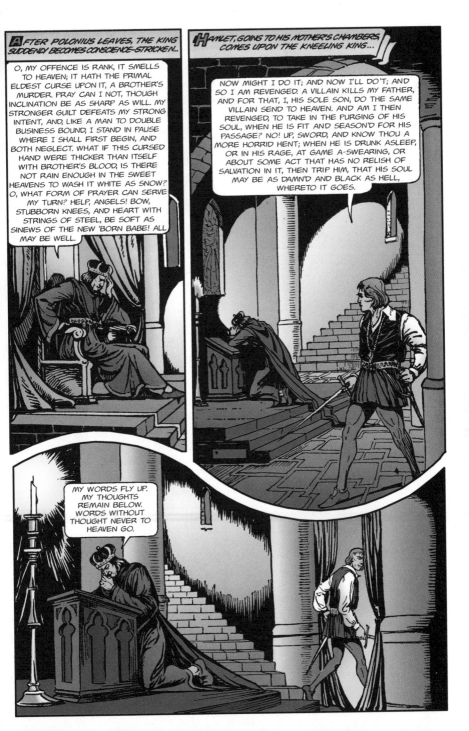

*TABLET BEARING THE COAT OF ARMS OF THE DEAD.

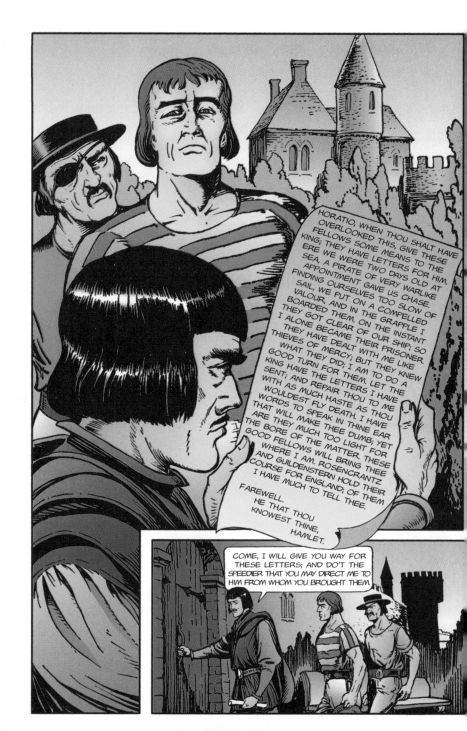

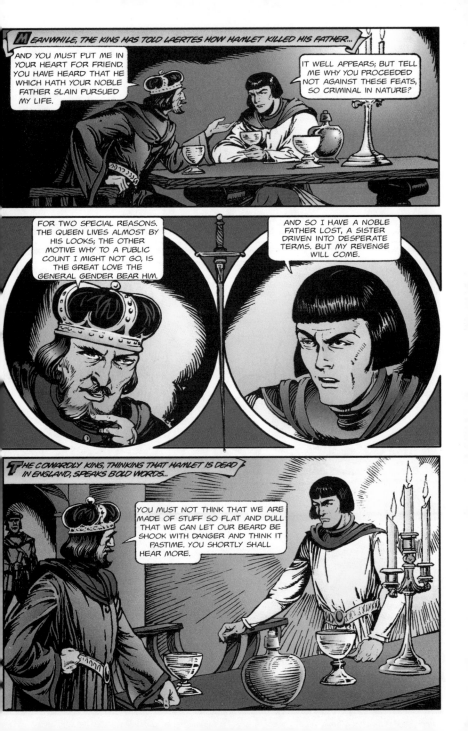

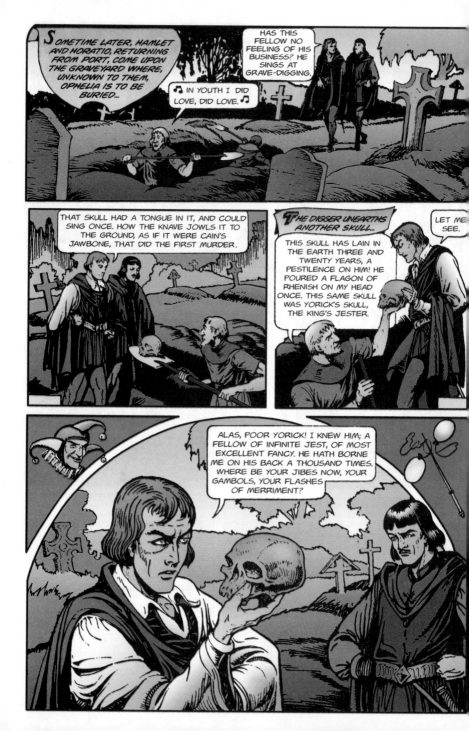

# HAMLET
## WILLIAM SHAKESPEARE

Murder, revenge, sex, politics, and a ghost—with ingredients like these, it's no wonder that *Hamlet* is one of the most famous of William Shakespeare's plays, and one of the most often performed. Some of Shakespeare's plays have gone in and out of fashion since his death *(A Midsummer Night's Dream* didn't appeal to audiences of the 19th Century, for example, and women in a late 20th-century audience are not likely to find *The Taming of the Shrew* as amusing as they might have in earlier times), but *Hamlet* has been with us steadily since the beginning.

## The Author

Not much is actually known—though much has been conjectured—about Shakespeare's life. He was born in 1564 in the English market town of Stratford-upon-Avon, and presumably (though there's no explicit record of it) attended the local grammar school. There he would have learned to read and write in English and, later, in Latin, the international language of diplomacy, theology, philosophy, politics, and science. In 1582 he married Anne Hathaway, who at 28 was ten years his senior (she was three months pregnant when they married, which might have had something to do with it). They had three children: a daughter, Susanna, in 1583, and twins, Hamnet and Judith, in 1585.

Exactly when Shakespeare left his wife and children in Stratford and went to live and work in London, and why he made such a move, nobody knows for certain. (The traditional story—that he had to leave Stratford because he got caught poaching deer on the estate of a local landowner, Sir Thomas Lucy—is entertaining but almost certainly not true.) All we really know is that by 1592 he was active enough in the London theater scene to be on the receiving end of a barbed attack by the playwright Robert Greene for daring to write blank verse and being "in his own conceit [opinion] the only Shakescene in a county."

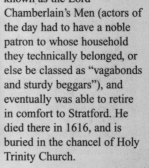

From the early 1590s through about 1612, Shakespeare lived in London, wrote plays, and prospered. He was both an actor and a shareholder in the acting company known as the Lord Chamberlain's Men (actors of the day had to have a noble patron to whose household they technically belonged, or else be classed as "vagabonds and sturdy beggars"), and eventually was able to retire in comfort to Stratford. He died there in 1616, and is buried in the chancel of Holy Trinity Church.

*Hamlet* was written and first performed during the period when England was moving from the Elizabethan era to the Jacobean. Elizabeth Tudor died in 1603, and James VI of Scotland came to the throne of England as James I. James was a Scot, the son of Elizabeth Tudor's cousin Mary, and he was nowhere near as charismatic and popular as his predecessor Elizabeth had been.

Elizabeth had ruled England for forty-five years, and had become almost a secular idol in the minds of her subjects. She wasn't just Elizabeth Tudor. She was Gloriana, the Virgin Queen, who said of herself, "I may have the body of a weak and feeble woman, but I have the heart and stomach of a King, and a King of England, too," and who said to her people, "Though you have had, and may have, many wiser princes sitting in this seat, yet you never had, nor shall have, any that will love you better." The

# The Elizabethan Stage

The theater in Elizabethan England was different, in several important ways, from the theater as we know it today. For one thing, the stage of the time wasn't like the one we're used to, in which the main area where the actors work is separated from the audience by an archway across which a curtain may be drawn. The main working area of a Shakespearean stage thrust out into the audience, who surrounded it on three sides—not surprisingly, the actors were much more involved with the members of the audience, often addressing them directly in asides and soliloquies (see sidebar), leading them in song, or having them assist in bits of business. (In one pre-Shakespearean play, an actor gives his cloak to a member of the audience to hold, and tells him, "since it is somewhat arrayed at the skirt/Whiles you do nothing, scrape of the dirt.")

Scenery was minimal to nonexistent. The skills of the playwright and of the actors served to indicate the setting and any changes of time or place. While this made for a bare stage much of the time, it also allowed the playwright to do fast-moving, far-ranging action that would have been impossible if elaborate scenery had needed to be taken away and brought out again between each scene and the next.

In addition to the architectural differences between modern and Elizabethan theaters, there were political differences as well. Freedom of the press as we know it today did not exist. Plays had to be licensed in order to be performed—but even the censorship was different from the modern variety. In a world where executions took place in public and bear-baiting (the killing of a staked-out bear by a pack of dogs) was a popular form of entertainment, sex and violence weren't likely to worry anybody very much. On the other hand, plays which contained seditious or treasonous material—or material which somebody high-ranking might happen to think was seditious or treasonous—could be denied a license.

This suppression of political discussion meant that plays dealing with political matters often did so by means of indirection. Playwrights would set the action in distant places and long-ago times (if you wanted to talk about tyranny, for example, Rome and Greece were always good), or they would use figura-

European rulers who were her contemporaries saw Elizabeth in a different but equally formidable aspect. Henry of Navarre, later King Henry IV of France, said of her admiringly, "She only is a king. She only knows how to rule!"

Elizabeth Tudor, in short, was going to be a hard act to follow, and James Stuart didn't look like he was the person to do it. He was a clumsy, unhandsome man, pathologically afraid of assassination—he wore thickly padded doublets to protect himself against knife attacks—and of attack by witchcraft. (He was also vehemently opposed to the new habit of smoking, calling it foul and unhealthful. He was dead right on that one, as it happens, but he didn't get any credit for it at the time, and smokers kept on polluting the air for almost four centuries before anybody raised the subject again.) James the First was no Gloriana; he had, instead, the dubious honor of being known as "the wisest fool in Christendom."

tive language and symbolism to clue the audience in to their political meanings.

The most famous difference between Elizabethan and modern drama is neither architectural nor political. It's the fact that while women had acted in the religious dramas of medieval England, and continued to act on the stage in Europe, all the female roles during this first great age of the English theater were played by men. Not until the reign of Charles II, in the second half of the next century, did women actors again take the stage in England.

Often the women's roles were played by boys. Shakespeare has Hamlet ask one of the "players" if his voice has broken yet: "Pray God your voice, like a piece of uncurrent gold [counterfeit money], be not cracked within the ring." Some of these boy-actors went on to take male roles later; others apparently specialized in female roles well into their twenties—which isn't surprising, considering that the female parts in many of Shakespeare's plays are demanding enough to tax the powers of a veteran actor, let alone a young and relatively new one. There's no reason to think, however, that these male actors were ineffective in their roles. A quick visit to the video rental shop to pick up *Tootsie* with Dustin Hoffman, *Mrs. Doubtfire* with Robin Williamson, or *The Crying Game* with Jaye Davidson, should be enough to dispel that notion.

## Hamlet, Prince of Denmark

The hero of Shakespeare's most famous tragedy is a complicated, puzzling character, renowned in world literature for his hesitation over the one big problem, but at the same time a man capable of acting swiftly—too swiftly in some cases—in lesser matters. He's a fast talker, able to dance verbal rings around people who aren't as quick on the uptake as he is; he's also a bit of an actor, and an unstoppable maker of puns and player with the double meanings of words. His wit is sharp, and not always kind. He suspects that the people around him are befriending him only in order to seek some advantage, he sometimes thinks about suicide, and he's prone to sudden mood shifts. He's not, at the moment, very tightly wrapped.

Hamlet is a young man; the play never gives his age exactly, but working it out from internal evidence he's probably no older than thirty, and many of his words and actions seem those of a man several years younger than that. He's an intellectual, a former student at the University of Wittenberg, in Germany—a school that in the sixteenth and early seventeenth centuries had an intellectual reputation somewhat like that of the University of California at Berkeley during the 1960s. Wittenberg was a hotbed of radical thought, notorious for both its real and its imaginary graduates. The Protestant reformer Martin Luther had gone to school there, and so had the fictional Doctor Faustus of pact-with-the-Devil fame (and protagonist, himself, of a tragedy by Elizabethan playwright Christopher Marlowe).

Many famous actors, over the years, have taken on the role of Hamlet. In the 18th century the most famous Hamlet was David Garrick, whose presentations of Shakespeare's plays at the Drury Lane theater in London helped to bring about a renewed popularity for the playwright. The first American to make his name in the role was Edwin Booth—whose fame as an actor was such that it even survived the fact that his younger brother, John Wilkes Booth, was the man who shot Abraham Lincoln. 20th century Hamlets on stage and in the movies include Laurence Olivier, Richard Burton, Richard Chamberlain, Derek Jacobi, and Mel Gibson.

ALAS, POOR YORICK! I KNEW HIM, A FELLOW OF INFINITE JEST, OF MOST EXCELLENT FANCY. HE HATH BORNE ME ON HIS BACK A THOUSAND TIMES. WHERE BE YOUR JIBES NOW, YOUR GAMBOLS, YOUR FLASHES OF MERRIMENT?

## Ophelia

Daughter of the King's aged advisor Polonius; sister to Laertes; and something not too clearly defined to Hamlet. Her father and brother talk to (and about) her alternately as though she is a sheltered innocent, and as though she's a woman of the world with a chance at making her family's fortune through Hamlet's attraction to her. Shakespeare's audience would not have regarded a marriage between Ophelia and Hamlet as impossible—Henry VIII had chosen English women of good but not royal family for four of his six wives. Nor would they have been surprised if Polonius had been almost as willing to see Ophelia become Hamlet's mistress as become his wife. The position of a mistress was less secure than that of a wife, but for the girl's family it promised almost as much power and wealth for as long as it lasted.

Ophelia, understandably, is getting mixed messages from all of this. She's not clear on whether her father and her brother want her to be a Good Girl, and hold out for marriage, or a Bad Girl, and hold out for as much as she can get. Hamlet, on the other hand, is making sexy small talk with her ("Lady, may I lie in your lap . . . I mean, my head in your lap," "that's a fair thought to lie between

TOMORROW IS ST. VALENTINE'S DAY, ALL IN THE MORNING BETIME, AND I A MAID AT YOUR WINDOW, TO BE YOUR VALENTINE.

maids' legs") when he isn't verbally abusing her ("I loved you not.")

Much as the members of her own family seem to vacillate between expecting Ophelia to be chaste and expecting her to be mercenary, Hamlet alternates between treating her as someone more virtuous than he is ("in thy orisons [prayers], be all my sins remembered"), and as someone who is next-door to a prostitute. Even his famous command "Get thee to a nunnery" had a double meaning in Elizabethan times: Besides retaining its literal meaning of a convent, a "nunnery" was a slang term for a whorehouse.

There's a distinct possibility that Ophelia and Hamlet were More Than Just Good Friends before the play starts. The songs she sings during her madness speak of seduction and betrayal, for example—"Quoth she 'Before you tumbled [had sex with] me, you promised me to wed.'" In any case, she's kept off balance by the conflicting messages she's getting from everybody around her, and when her boyfriend (possibly her lover) kills her father and then is himself banished from the kingdom, the blow knocks her off-center for good.

## Polonius

The aged advisor to the king of Denmark. As the noted writer and critic Samuel Johnson (1709-1784) said in his *Notes on Shakespeare*: "Polonius is a man bred in courts, exercised in business, stored with observation, confident in his knowledge, proud of his eloquence, and declining into dotage. . . ."

# Close to the Throne

The role of advisor to the king was one that Shakespeare's audience would easily have recognized. The Tudor monarchs of the century just past had been particularly well-served by a whole series of great advisors. Henry VIII had Cardinal Wolsey; Elizabeth I claimed the loyalty of men like Francis Walsingham and William Cecil. When making Cecil her Principal Secretary, Elizabeth said to him: "This judgment I have of you, that you will not be corrupted with any manner of gift; and you will be faithful to the State; and without respect of my private will, you will give me that counsel that you think best." Such an expression of confidence, coming from an absolute monarch, was no light thing.

The royal counselors of the 16th century were subtle, intelligent men, university-educated in a day when even great nobles often had only a few years of schooling, and their duties ranged from the making of foreign and domestic policy to the selection of prospective royal brides and bridegrooms—often with a bit of espionage and counterintelligence on the side. (None of the great Tudor advisors ever lurked in person behind an arras to eavesdrop on a conversation—at least, not that we know of!—but any one of them could have sent somebody else to do it and not felt a quiver of conscience afterward.) A man who aspired to such a position was one who wanted to climb high, and who was not deterred by the often deadly price of failure.

As such a man, Polonius is the representative of a day that was already beginning to pass when Hamlet was written. Elizabeth Tudor was dying, and members of the Stuart dynasty, who would rule England for a good part of the next century, had in general a much poorer track record at choosing advisors. In his prime, working for Prince Hamlet's father, Polonius must have been hot stuff indeed. Now, however, his position at court has grown uncertain. He is unsure of his influence over the new king; and the heir to the throne, young Hamlet, holds him in visible contempt.

Such a man is positive and confident, because he knows that his mind was once strong, and knows not that it is become weak."

Polonius labors to make himself indispensable to Claudius and Gertrude, and strives to exploit the relationship between his daughter and Prince Hamlet. He snoops incessantly: the fatal episode behind Gertrude's curtains is only the last. Before that, he's aided Claudius to spy on Hamlet, and has even dispatched a servant to check up on his own son Laertes at school in Paris:

*"Inquire me first what Danskers*
*[Danes] are in Paris;*
*And how, and who, what means, and*
*where they keep,*
*What company, at what expense;*
*and finding*
*By this encompassment and drift of*
*question [roundabout inquiry]*
*That they do know my son,*
*come you more nearer*
*Than your particular demands will*
*touch it [you will come closer than*
*you would by direct questioning].*

The thing about Polonius is that none of his advice is actually bad. It's full of the tried and true procedures for whatever problem he believes he's applying it to. The difficulty is that the situation itself has gotten completely out of hand. Matters are no longer what they seem, and the king's chief advisor isn't on top of things any more. The audience knows this, even if Polonius doesn't: as advisor to the old king, Polonius should have known about Claudius's plans in advance, and should have dealt with them. When the biggest test in his career came along, he missed the vital clues, and failed. If he'd been doing his job properly in the first place, there would have been no need for a ghost to appear to young Hamlet and set the events of the play into motion.

### Laertes

Son of Polonius and brother of Ophelia. He's young and hot-blooded—no critic has ever accused him of delaying his actions for too long, or of thinking about them too much. He's easily manipulated by people like Claudius, who are brighter and more subtle than he is.

### Horatio

Friend of Hamlet, and a fellow student from his Wittenberg days. Horatio isn't really a participant in the events of the drama; his main purpose is to be somebody whom Hamlet trusts, and in whom Hamlet can confide. He is the play's "normal" character, who stands in for the members of the audience. In the court of Denmark,

where everybody—even Hamlet himself—has a hidden agenda, or is working some kind of angle, Horatio is a rarity, an honest man who really is what he seems to be.

### Gertrude

Queen of Denmark. Hamlet's mother; widow of Old Hamlet, wife of King Claudius. Marrying one's brother's widow was a dubious thing, theologically, during the middle ages and the renaissance. In the early part of the 16th Century, when Henry VIII's marriage to Catherine of Aragon failed to produce a male heir, Henry became convinced that the cause of the failure was Catherine's previous marriage to his older brother Arthur, who had died while still Prince of Wales. At the same time, such marriages between in-laws often took place for political reasons—as had also been the case with Henry VIII and Catherine of Aragon.

As long as Old Hamlet's death is believed to have been from natural causes, the hasty marriage of Claudius and Gertrude can be viewed by political observers as an act designed to insure stability at Elsinore during a time of crisis. (The crisis is the threatened invasion of Denmark by young Fortinbras, intent on revenging the death of his father, Old Fortinbras, at the hands of Old

Hamlet.) The theological problem remains, however, and Hamlet probably isn't the only person in Denmark who regards the marriage as at least technically incestuous.

Gertrude herself is a kindhearted but unintellectual woman, more ruled by her emotions and her sensual desires than by anything else. She doesn't seem to know about Claudius's murder of her first husband; the ghost itself exempts her from its call for revenge, and Hamlet's cutting remarks and wild actions rouse concern in her rather than suspicion of his motives. As the literary critic Northrop Frye said of her, "One reason why it's Gertrude, rather than Claudius, who drives Hamlet up the wall is her total unconsciousness of having done anything wrong . . . . Hamlet does not see that the instinct to hang on his father was the same one that prompted her to attach herself after his death to the nearest strong-looking man who presented himself."

### Claudius

King of Denmark. Brother to Old Hamlet; husband of Gertrude; Hamlet's uncle. He has killed his brother, Old Hamlet, by means of an undetectable poison, and now has possession both of Old Hamlet's kingdom, and of his wife. Which of the two Claudius wanted more, and which was the desire that prompted him to murder, is never told to the audience.

Like some of Shakespeare's other villains—Macbeth, for example—Claudius is a good (or at least potentially good) man trapped in bad circumstances. He has a conscience, and he recognizes his actions as evil—as he says in his prayer, they "smell to heaven." Nor does he try to kill Hamlet until it becomes clear that Hamlet is trying to kill him; that is, not until after Hamlet stabs Polonius through the arras (not to mention through the spleen, kidneys, and liver). After that point Claudius acts in self-defense. His prime motivation seems to be the preservation of civil order in Denmark, and the protection of the kingdom against foreign invasion.

Claudius is an intelligent man—he gets the point of Hamlet's punning insults, and he quickly figures out what's up with the "Mousetrap" (Hamlet's play-within-the-play, designed to "catch the conscience of the king")—and he is a bold man, acting promptly upon his insights. He is Hamlet's true adversary, and much more the Prince's mental equal than a hotheaded boy like Laertes could ever be.

### Rosencrantz and Guildenstern

A pair of Hamlet's old friends, summoned by the King and Queen to jolly him out of his depression (and, if they can't do that, to figure out what's going on with him). They stand in sharp contrast to Horatio, Hamlet's true confidant, since they are, in fact, willing to betray the prince's friendship. Hamlet sees through them at once, and eventually disposes of them offstage, by rather cold-bloodedly substituting their names for his in the letter of execution they were carrying to England.

### The Ghost

The spirit of Old Hamlet, the previous King of Denmark and the father of the Prince—unless it's

something else. (Curiously, there is a long-standing tradition in the theater that Shakespeare himself played the part of the Ghost in the first performances of the play.)

### Fortinbras

Prince of Norway, as Hamlet is Prince of Denmark. He's a minor character, not mentioned in the Classics Illustrated adaptation and omitted from many theatrical productions, but he's an important one just the same. He is a man of action to Hamlet's man of thought. Old Hamlet, Prince Hamlet's father, killed Old Fortinbras, Prince Fortinbras's father, and took some Norwegian land some time before the play began. Now Fortinbras is seeking to avenge his father's death by retaking that land. This feared invasion is the reason that the double watches are being kept on the walls of Elsinore, putting guards in position to see the Ghost. The possible invasion may also be the reason why Claudius married Gertrude in such unseemly haste. And at the end of the play, after the death of the entire royal house of Denmark, it is Fortinbras who takes over the country, arriving just after Hamlet has breathed his last. He speaks the last line of the play "Go, bid the soldiers shoot," once he has summed up the action and tied up the last loose ends.

Over the centuries since *Hamlet* was written, students of literature have been attracted to the play because it's so rich in "problems"— points which can be argued and analyzed and approached from many different directions. Here's a sampling of some of those "problems."

## The Plot

### The Problem of the Ghost

*What is the real nature of the Ghost? Is it in fact the spirit of the dead king, or is it some kind of supernatural (and probably demonic) being? And is it even telling the truth?*

It's difficult for modern audiences to appreciate just how serious a problem the Ghost and its call to vengeance pose for Hamlet. Since we don't (most of us) believe either in ghosts or in the need for private justice, our tendency is to accept the ghost at face value as a plot device, and therefore spend the rest of the play wondering why Hamlet doesn't just get on with the revenge business.

Shakespeare's audience, however, believed both in ghosts and demons. Likewise, revenge—while certainly not a part of everybody's daily life— was still an open matter for debate. From Hamlet's point of view, the ghost is a real thing, no question; the difficulty lies in determining what kind of a real thing. (Note that the ghost is seen first by the soldiers on the

wall, and later by the solidly normal and rational Horatio, before Hamlet ever lays eyes on it.)

The very first time Hamlet addresses the ghost, he makes his doubts and worries plain:

*"Be thou a spirit of health or goblin damned,*
*Bring with thee airs from heaven or blasts from hell,*
*Be thy intents wicked or charitable,*
*Thou com'st in such a questionable [problematic] shape*
*That I will speak to thee."*

This is, in fact, the whole difficulty in a nutshell. The specter on the battlements of Elsinore may indeed be Hamlet's father's ghost, telling a true story and calling on his son to do his duty as heir to the throne. If the ghost is real and speaks truth, then an act of murder is going unpunished, and Hamlet, as a member of the royal family, is perhaps the only person at court highly placed enough to carry out justice. If the ghost's story is true, the current ruler of the kingdom has no real right to the throne—a state of affairs which, given the almost mystical identity believed to exist between monarch and kingdom, could have serious consequences for everyone in Denmark.

Neither Hamlet nor Shakespeare's audience, however, could afford to forget the other possibility: that the apparition which appeared on the castle battlements was not a true ghost, but a demon from Hell taking on a ghostly form in order to tempt the Prince of Denmark into the sin of murder. Hamlet sums up the problem, for himself and for the audience, when he decides to use the visiting troupe of actors to set up a test of the king's guilt:

*"... The spirit that I have seen*
*May be a devil, and the devil hath power*
*T'assume a pleasing shape; yea, and perhaps,*
*Out of my weakness and my melancholy,*
*As he is very potent with such spirits,*
*Abuses me to damn me.*

THAT NIGHT, ACCOMPANIED BY HORATIO AND MARCELLUS, HAMLET GOES TO MEET THE GHOST. EXACTLY AT MIDNIGHT THE GHOST APPEARS...

ANGELS AND MINISTERS OF GRACE DEFEND US! BE THOU A SPIRIT OF HEALTH OR GOBLIN DAMN'D, BRING WITH THEE AIRS FROM HEAVEN OR BLASTS FROM HELL, BE THY INTENTS WICKED OR CHARITABLE, THOU COM'ST IN SUCH A QUESTIONABLE SHAPE THAT I WILL SPEAK TO THEE. I'LL CALL THEE HAMLET, KING, FATHER, ROYAL DANE--O, ANSWER ME! WHAT MAY THIS MEAN, THAT THOU, DEAD CORSE', AGAIN IN COMPLETE STEEL REVISITS THUS?

CORPSE'

*I'll have grounds*
*More relative [pertinent;*
*    convincing] than this. The play's the*
*    thing*
*Wherein I'll catch the conscience*
*    of the King."*

Later, just before the performance, he tells Horatio the same thing:

*"Observe my uncle. If his occulted*
*    [hidden] guilt*
*Do not itself unkennel in one speech,*
*It is a damned ghost that we have*
*    seen,*
*And my imaginations are as foul*
*As Vulcan's stithy [forge]."*

If we go by the beliefs of the day, several things argue in favor of the demonic theory: The ghost is visibly offended when Horatio orders it to speak "by Heaven;" it vanishes when the cock crows; it is an angry spirit, and comes to Hamlet armed and armored; and it speaks from beneath the ground, the traditional abode of demons and evil spirits. Most important-ly, the ghost urges Hamlet toward committing a deed which would at worst be murder and regi-cide, and which even at best would involve taking on a task which rightfully belonged to God alone.

Given these conflicting possibilities, and given how much is at stake (nothing less than the health of the state of Denmark and of his own immortal soul) Hamlet is impelled to look for out-side confirmation of the Ghost's accusations. Hence the "Mousetrap," the play-

within-the play depicting the murder of a king by his brother, which Hamlet uses as a sort of psychologi-cal test.

## Revenge, Regicide, and Usurpation

*Why doesn't Hamlet act promptly to avenge his father, as Fortinbras does, and as Laertes does when he hears of the death of Polonius?*

At the time Shakespeare was writ-ing *Hamlet* (and re-writing *Hamlet*; there seem to have been at least three different versions put on by the Lord Chamberlain's Men between 1599 and 1603, with no way for us to determine which one was the author's "preferred cut") revenge was a popu-lar literary device. Most people, how-ever, accepted the idea that seeking revenge was a sin; vengeance belonged to God and justice belonged to the State. Private justice might have been necessary in "the old days," or in barbarous countries like Scotland or Italy or Spain, but proper Englishmen had lawyers and judges to settle their problems for them. Revenge—intended, planned, and carried out—was a killing in cold blood, and unlikely to gain the complete sympathy of an English audience no mat-ter how much it enter-tained them.

Furthermore, even if the Ghost is what it seems to be, and is speaking truth, Hamlet still faces no light problem. Claudius may be the murderer of Hamlet's father, but he is also the King of Denmark and not just any common or gar-den variety villain. The

AFTER POLONIUS LEAVES, THE KING SUDDENLY BECOMES CONSCIENCE-STRICKEN.

O, MY OFFENCE IS RANK, IT SMELLS TO HEAVEN; IT HATH THE PRIMAL ELDEST CURSE UPON IT, A BROTHER'S MURDER. PRAY CAN I NOT, THOUGH INCLINATION BE AS SHARP AS WILL. MY STRONGER GUILT DEFEATS MY STRONG INTENT, AND, LIKE A MAN TO DOUBLE BUSINESS BOUND, I STAND IN PAUSE WHERE I SHALL FIRST BEGIN, AND BOTH NEGLECT. WHAT IF THIS CURSED HAND WERE THICKER THAN ITSELF WITH BROTHER'S BLOOD, IS THERE NOT RAIN ENOUGH IN THE SWEET HEAVENS TO WASH IT WHITE AS SNOW? O, WHAT FORM OF PRAYER CAN SERVE MY TURN? HELP, ANGELS! BOW, STUBBORN KNEES, AND HEART WITH STRINGS OF STEEL, BE SOFT AS SINEWS OF THE NEW 'BORN BABE! ALL MAY BE WELL.

problem of regicide (literally, "king-killing") was a hot topic in Shakespeare's day. In a period when monarchs ruled for life, and ruled absolutely, killing the king was often the only way to bring about changes at the top. At the same time, kings were not, in the mind of the day, ordinary men. When Claudius tells Gertrude, "There's such divinity doth hedge a king," he means it—the king is not God, but is God-like in a worldly sense, and stands in relation to the kingdom as God does to the universe as a whole.

Killing a king, or killing a ruling queen, was not just murder but a kind of sacrilege, a religious as well as a civil crime. Not that this had ever stopped people from trying: Elizabeth I had often been the target of assassination plots, as had James I—whose father, Henry Lord Darnley, had been killed by Earl Bothwell, and whose mother, Mary Queen of Scots, was herself imprisoned and, ultimately, executed by order of her cousin Elizabeth.

Closely related to the problem of regicide was the problem of usurpation—the stealing of the kingship from the rightful heir by another claimant. English history gives us a number of instances of such royal theft. Henry VII, the founder of the Tudor dynasty, took over the throne after defeating Richard III at the Battle of Bosworth Field; and Richard III may or may not have come to the throne illicitly himself, after first declaring the two sons of his brother Edward IV illegitimate, and then having them murdered.

A number of Shakespeare's plays deal with themes of regicide and usurpation—*Richard II*, *Julius Caesar*, and *Macbeth*, to name only three of them—and other plays such as *The Tempest*, *King Lear*, and *As You Like It* feature deposed or dispossessed dukes and princes. Getting rid of a bad or incompetent king, by whatever means, was a matter for intense intellectual debate all through the 16th and 17th centuries. Eventually, debate changed to action. In 1649, James's son, Charles I, would be executed by the English Parliament at the end of a nasty civil war, and the "divinity [that] doth hedge a king" would never be the same again.

### Kingship in Denmark: Why Claudius, Anyway?

*If Hamlet's father, Old Hamlet, was king of Denmark, why is Uncle Claudius the king now instead of Hamlet, and why doesn't anybody—including Hamlet—seem especially resentful of this?*

Some readers of the play may wonder why, if Prince Hamlet was the old king's grown son, the throne of Denmark has gone to Claudius in the first place. Nobody at the Danish court seems to regard Claudius's ascension to the title as illegitimate (at least, as long as Old Hamlet's death was a natural one). Even Hamlet, who might be expected to think so, is from the moment we first meet him far more worried about his mother's sudden remarriage than about any threat to his own ambitions. The most resentful remarks he makes about Claudius-as-king (that Claudius has "popp'd in between the election and my hopes") are pale condemnation next to the epithets he reserves for Claudius as husband of Gertrude and possible murderer of Old Hamlet:

*. . . Bloody, bawdy villain!*
*Remorseless, treacherous, lecherous,*
   *kindless villain!*

The implication in the play is that the crown of Denmark doesn't necessarily go in a direct line from father to son, but to an heir drawn from a number of eligible prospects—of whom Claudius, as the brother of the old king, would certainly have been one. (This would be the "election" of which Hamlet speaks; he uses the word in its old sense to refer to a choice, rather than to any kind of modern democratic process.) Exactly who would have done the choosing isn't made clear; Shakespeare's interest in the political structure of a highly-fictionalized Denmark doesn't go much farther than necessary for his story.

However, there are good reasons why Claudius rather than Prince Hamlet might have gotten the nod: the desire to have an older and more experienced man in charge of the kingdom at a time of crisis; the fact that Claudius was there and available at the critical moment; even the fact that Claudius was able and willing to marry the widow of the old king, and in that fashion provide the kingdom with yet another assurance of stability and continuity. It's even possible that the old king had at some point indicated his preference for Claudius as an heir, in the same fashion as the dying Hamlet speaks for Fortinbras ("th' election lights/On Fortinbras; he has my dying voice.")

## Melancholy, Madness, and Humors

*How much of Hamlet's madness is real, and how much of it is pretense, the "antic disposition" he tells his friends he will put on, in order to deceive the king? (Hamlet asserts "I am but mad north-northwest." Does this mean, "Don't worry; I'm only faking madness," or does it mean, "Be warned; there's at least one subject out there on which I am not entirely rational"?)*

Hamlet feigns a genuine insanity, seeking in that way to throw off any suspicions that Claudius may have about him—but how much of his faked madness is a cover for real mental disturbance? This question has fascinated critics and actors for generations, because it's quite clear that Hamlet is, at the very least, seriously troubled. What kind of mental trouble he's suffering from is another matter. Something in the character of Hamlet seems to speak to every generation, so that whatever the favorite mental disturbance of the day, the Prince of Denmark will be described by someone as suffering from it.

Even within the play itself, theories about Hamlet's condition go back and forth. Polonius is at first convinced that the Prince is suffering from love-sickness, itself regarded a form of madness. For love of Ophelia, Polonius says, Hamlet

*". . . fell into a sadness, then into a*
   *fast,*
*Thence to a watch [insomnia], thence*
   *into a weakness,*
*Thence to a lightness, and, by this*
   *declension,*
*Into the madness wherein now he*
   *raves . . . ."*

Hamlet, at the same time, makes references to "my weakness and my melancholy." In late Renaissance medical theory, the human body and

# Hamlet's Soliloquies

If Hamlet isn't crazy (or at least, isn't crazy all of the time), then why does he talk to himself so much? The answer lies in the conventions—the accepted ways for showing things—of the Elizabethan stage. Actors could indicate a change of time or place for the audience by talking about it, and have the description accepted as part of the dialogue, even though people in everyday conversation seldom bother to describe their surroundings to each other. Likewise, the audience would accept that a character might speak to them directly, either in brief comments (known as "asides") made during conversations with other characters, or in longer speeches made while the character was alone on the stage ("soliloquies").

A character's asides are "heard" only by the audience, even though other characters may be on the stage at the time. Soliloquies, also, are heard in this fashion—some of them were in fact addressed to the audience directly. The invisible wall between the characters and the audience was not then as high and thick as it later became. Another convention of the aside and the soliloquy is that the character who's speaking is telling the truth, and that his or her words can be trusted to a higher degree than words spoken between characters.

In none of Shakespeare's plays are soliloquies more important than in *Hamlet*. One of Hamlet's main problems is determining how and what he should think about a particular thing, the death of his father. The use of the soliloquy technique allows Shakespeare to give the audience a glimpse of Hamlet thinking, and lets him make the process of thought into something dramatically interesting. Also, the soliloquies emphasize Hamlet's lonely and isolated role at the court of Denmark. He must keep a close watch over his tongue, and not say anything he doesn't intend to say (and in fact, most of what Hamlet does say in public has multiple meanings—sharp, rather nasty jokes and puns). When he's alone, therefore, it's not surprising that his speech becomes wild and overwrought in reaction to the sudden freedom.

mind were ruled by the four "humors"—blood, phlegm, yellow bile (also known as choler), and black bile—each of which had a corresponding physical and mental type associated with it. Melancholy was caused by an excess of black bile in the system. Symptoms included brooding, inactivity, and a lack of interest in the affairs of the world.

In later centuries, other mental ailments were put forward as the source of Hamlet's problems. No sooner had Freudian psychology discovered the Oedipus complex (according to which a son will on some unconscious level be in love with his mother, and hate his father for being the main rival for her affection), than Hamlet was promptly diagnosed as being Oedipal. His scene with Gertrude in Act III, Scene iv, considered in that light, at once took on all sorts of sexual overtones that directors and actors had never glimpsed in it before.

These days, one suspects, Hamlet might be regarded as suffering from depression. He's certainly under a lot of mental stress, even before he meets the ghost, and his behavior is odd enough to worry Gertrude and Claudius both (though possibly for different reasons).

## "Now Might I Do It Pat"

*Why doesn't Hamlet kill Claudius after the play-within-a-play, when he finds the King praying? Claudius's guilt is as firmly established at that point as it's ever going to be, and Hamlet has got a clear opportunity.*

Hamlet, after the success of his play-within-a-play stratagem, comes across King Claudius at prayer, and—like everybody else in the play when given a similar opportunity—decides to eavesdrop. Sneakiness is its own reward; Claudius comes right out and says to God what not even the mental shock of Hamlet's "Mousetrap" could make him say in front of witnesses:

*O, my offense is rank, it smells to heaven;*
*It has the primal eldest curse upon't,*
*A brother's murder. Pray can I not,*
*Though inclination be as strong as will.*

Why does Hamlet, when presented with proof of his suspicions and a vulnerable target for immediate revenge, decide not to run Claudius through with his rapier then and there? (Instead, he lets himself get sidetracked into haranguing his bewildered mother about her sex life, and, eventually, into killing Polonius by mistake.) One possible answer is the one which Hamlet himself gives:

*. . . And am I then revenged*
*To take him in the purging of his soul,*
*When he is fit and seasoned for his passage?*

The concept of "immortal vengeance"—of not only killing the body of the person being revenged upon, but of damning his soul as well—was a popular one in the revenge plays. In its milder forms, the idea was to take out the human target under circumstances which would make it impossible for him to confess his sins before death. Hamlet alludes to this, as well:

*When he is drunk asleep, or in his rage,*
*Or in th' incestuous pleasure of his bed,*
*At game a-swearing, or about some act*
*That has no relish of salvation in't—*
*Then trip him, that his heels may kick at heaven,*
*And that his soul may be as damned and black*
       *As hell, whereto it goes.*

MY WORDS FLY UP, MY THOUGHTS REMAIN BELOW. WORDS WITHOUT THOUGHT NEVER TO HEAVEN GO.

In its extreme forms, the avenger might actually force or trick his victim into committing a mortal sin, then kill him immediately afterward. For example, in the play *Alphonsus, Emperor of Germany*, written around 1594, the Spanish villain, Alexander, tricks Alphonsus into forswearing God, and then kills him, shouting, "Die and be damn'd! Now am I satisfied!"

At this point, of course, the avenger in the play has become almost as much of a moral disaster area as his victim. Hamlet never goes that far, and even the reasons he gives himself for delaying vengeance—while coming from the standard revenge-tragedy mold—sound a bit false in the mouth of the character whom we've been watching and listening to, by now, for two and a half acts. In a play as full of psychological subtlety and character insight as *Hamlet*, it's hard not to suspect a certain amount of rationalization on Hamlet's part. As Northrop Frye said, "Among the conflict of emotions in his mind when he watches Claudius praying and wonders if he should kill him now, one is undoubtedly a strong distaste for a treacherous and rather cowardly act, which is what sticking a rapier into a man's turned back really amounts to, whatever the urgency of the revenge ethic."

*Hamlet* is a play full of doubles: double meanings and double-dealing, and characters who, like Rosencrantz and Guildenstern, often come in doubles as well. From Marcellus and Bernardo, the two soldiers who first spy the ghost of Old Hamlet on the castle

wall, all the way down to the pair of portraits Hamlet talks about in his confrontation with his mother Gertrude, things and people in *Hamlet* appear in pairs.

Hamlet himself, standing as he does at the center of his play, makes a pair with any one of a number of other characters. First, and perhaps the most obvious, is the pairing with his dead father, also named Hamlet. After that we can match him with his friend Horatio, who shares the prince's intelligence and his thoughtful mind, and who is in some ways a picture of what Hamlet might have been like if things had not gone wrong. Then there's Laertes, a student at Paris as Hamlet was a student at Wittenberg, whose headlong actions and unthinking emotionalism contrast with Hamlet's almost too-reflective behavior; and the briefly-met Fortinbras, a complete man of action, who shares with both Hamlet and Laertes the problem of what to do about the person who's killed your father. And finally there is Claudius, King to Hamlet's Prince, who also holds the double position of Hamlet's stepfather and his uncle.

Another powerful set of symbols in *Hamlet* has to do with images of rot, decay, corruption, and weeds. At the very beginning of the play, it is the judgment of the soldier, Marcellus,

AFTER A FEW MOMENTS OF SPARRING, LAERTES FINALLY BREAKS THROUGH HAMLET'S DEFENSE. BUT INSTEAD OF SIMPLY BEING HIT, HAMLET IS ASTOUNDED AND INFURIATED TO FIND THAT HE HAS BEEN WOUNDED BY AN UNTIPPED FOIL. HE NOW REALIZES LAERTES' TRUE INTENT AND RUSHES MADLY AT HIS OPPONENT. AS THEY SCUFFLE, THEY BOTH DROP THEIR FOILS. IN THE ENSUING CONFUSION, THEY MISTAKENLY EXCHANGE FOILS.

PART THEM; THEY ARE INCENS'D.

NAY, COME AGAIN.